The Sacral Chakra

ALSO BY MIRTHA CONTRERAS

The Root Chakra

El Chakra Raíz

The Sacral Chakra
Healing the Center of Sex, Creativity, Pleasure and Joy

Learn To Heal Yourself With Your Energy
(The Healing Energy Series)

by Mirtha Contreras

a **CHESTNUT HILL WRITING** book

published by CreateSpace Independent Publishing Platform

Contents

Before We Start - A Few Words about Our Evolving Self and the Chakra System

Our soul's main goal is to evolve, and one of the ways it does this is by overcoming the challenges we face in our daily lives. What does this mean? That human life is not static - it is in constant motion and it's natural for certain life cycles to end in order to open the door to new ones. For example, many physical, mental, and emotional changes occur as we grow from children into teenagers and then adults.

When we begin to feel uncomfortable, dissatisfied, and unhappy in work, romantic, or everyday life, we know it's time for one life cycle to end and another to begin. It's then that our inner self perceives that our current situation no longer serves us and requests a change. So we begin the journey to heal, to change things within ourselves so that change can come about in our physical world.

Note that the end of a cycle does not necessarily mean that we must terminate a given situation. In other words, it doesn't mean you need to dump your boyfriend, get a divorce, or quit your job. While some situations may call for drastic measures, others require a simple change in direction or some kind of refocus. For example, a couple in a long-term relationship may feel like their relationship isn't really moving forward. To get over this problem, they might move in together. This is one way a relationship may change its course.

If, on the other hand, we ignore the shouts for change coming from our inner self, our mental, emotional, and physical bodies suffer until we are forced to make the necessary changes. If we do not make these changes, we will inevitably repeat certain patterns or scripts in our lives until we stop and ask ourselves: "What's going on? Why do I always attract the same kind of partner? Why do I always have problems with my boss? Why does this always happen to me?"

So we go through life making changes and transforming ourselves. As we go through the different stages of our lives, new needs and challenges arise and we desire new experiences. That is our nature: when a lesson is learned, we move on to the next level. That is how we heal, grow, and evolve.

When we are really alert and pay attention to what shows up in our lives, becoming conscious of our reality, the changes and transformations necessary for our evolution will also become apparent.

As you may recall from the first book of this series (*The Root Chakra*), I explained that human beings have several bodies (physical, emotional, mental, and energetic). As you learned, the energetic body is comprised of the aura and the chakra system. And it is via those energy centers - called chakras - that life energy travels through our being.

Throughout this book (and the others in this series), we will focus on the seven major chakras and how these energy centers can help us - each one according to its specific function - to bring healing, growth, and evolution to our lives. The chakras help us to heal and evolve. How? They manifest in our daily lives to show us what we need to change.

Energy moves through these seven energy centers in sequential order, beginning with the most basic: the First Chakra represents survival, which has to do with our basic desire for what we need to live (food, shelter, clothing, health, companionship).

From there, energy travels to the Second Chakra, which connects us with feelings - with our emotions and desires - and that which gives us joy and pleasure.

The need for survival, coupled with the desire to feel pleasure and want more, inevitably connects us with our Power (Third Chakra). That power activates our drive, moves us into action, and empowers us to say to life: "I can do it."

And by affirming to life that "yes, I can do it," life energy moves to the Fourth Chakra, and we begin to love ourselves unconditionally. Now we can treat ourselves and others with love, compassion, and respect. The energy of giving and receiving flows harmoniously and our self-esteem is restored.

When we experience loving feelings and the desire to give and receive, we want to express them. The energy that comes from the Fourth Chakra can be transformed into many forms of expression, bringing us to the Fifth Chakra.

At this point we begin to have a very intimate connection with our inner self and, suddenly, it's easy to see things from another perspective. Instead of merely observing the world that surrounds us, we allow ourselves to look beyond what we see in the physical world. When this communion with our inner self happens, we are in tune with the Sixth Chakra.

Then, finally, we begin to understand that we are not alone - that somehow we are all connected - and that there is a higher wisdom that loves us and supports our soul in its healing, growth, and evolution. With this realization, our Seventh Chakra becomes balanced.

Introduction

Remember that the chakras are energy centers where the Kundalini energy makes its way from the Root Chakra to the Crown Chakra. What is their function? They strive to keep our energy body balanced and, by resonance, our energy body is balanced with the mental, emotional, and physical bodies.

When one or more of these energy centers is not balanced because we hold thoughts or emotions that do not generate well-being, energy stagnates and does not flow through our system. This has negative effects on our mental, emotional and physical bodies, and may make us restless or ill.

In this, the second book of this series, we will discuss the Second Chakra, which is also called *Sacral, Holy, Svadhisthana, Hara,* or *Tanteen.*

The Sacral Chakra is aligned with the spine and located above the pubic bone, about three or four fingers below the navel. When the Sacral Chakra is vibrating at the frequency that corresponds to its optimal performance, it shines with a bright, intense orange color. When this occurs, the Kundalini energy can move smoothly to the next chakra.

This energy center allows us to relate to life through *emotions.* Its key phrase is "I *feel,*" and it is the seat of creative energy and everything that has to do with our sexuality.

We can also associate this chakra with changes as it is related to hormonal changes that affect our emotional and mental bodies. The Second Chakra is also associated with movement, pleasure, empathy, creativity, productivity, and sociability. The function of this chakra is to provide pleasure and to help us enjoy life with all five of our senses. As I mentioned before, it relates to desire and sexuality, as well as procreation, conception, and pregnancy. Finally, it also has to do with relationships and appreciation for beautiful things.

When balanced and harmonious, this chakra enables us to love life and to connect with it from a feeling of pleasure.

PART I – UNDERSTANDING YOUR SACRAL CHAKRA

What Is the Sacral Chakra? What Does It Mean to Us?

The Sacral Chakra is the seat of your conscious, creative, and pleasure-seeking self. Hedonistic in nature, it governs all our primal impulses and kindles passion for life. In harmony, the Sacral Chakra encourages the development of our personal identity, manages emotional stability, and promotes healthy relationships.

The Sanskrit name for this chakra is "*Swadhisthana*," which can be divided into "swadi," meaning "one's own" and "adhisthana," meaning "the place of residence." It is the place that houses the ego and sense of self, where all mental impressions, or "Samkaras," are stored. Our perception of the world is shaped by the past experiences held in this chakra. All feelings, emotions, and primal instincts originate within the Sacral Chakra. The "gut feeling" is one way that the Sacral Chakra communicates to us. It can warn us of danger, arouse sexual curiosity, and communicate our deeper feelings to us.

To view the lovely image of the Sacral Chakra in full color, please visit:

http://OpenYourChakras.com/SacralChakra_lotus

Physically, the Sacral Chakra is located two inches below the belly button, in the center depth of the gut. It governs the lower back, hips, sacrum, pelvis, sexual and reproductive organs, urinary tract, kidneys, adrenal glands, spleen, liver, appendix, intestines, and joints. It's associated with the color orange and the element water, because the energy flows smoothly like a channel when it's balanced. When the Sacral Chakra is imbalanced, energy pools up and stagnates like a swamp.

The Sacral Chakra determines our capacity for embracing the pleasures of life and our motivation to act. It gives us the tools to unlock our individual purpose and actually have a good time doing it! The Sacral Chakra possesses these attributes for the purpose of individual satisfaction and fulfillment.

SEX

This chakra is directly intertwined with relationships - the relationships between you and your family members, friends, and lovers. The more open and free-flowing the Sacral Chakra, the more you can give and embrace love. You are comfortable with yourself, your body, and your sexuality and you have a healthy sexual appetite.

As this chakra is the storehouse for mental impressions, it also stores the memories past sexual encounters. It is a sensitive area that determines our levels of trust, communication and how far we are willing to go. The Sacral Chakra raises the appropriate boundaries so that we don't get into the habit of either giving ourselves too freely or closing ourselves off completely.

CREATIVITY

The Sacral Chakra is the abode of your creative self. It fosters the creative force behind our originality and helps us bring forth the full essence our personality. It contains an organizing power that allows you to collect yourself, muster all the unique abilities you possess, and create something original and sincere.

PASSION

Passion fuels creation. It's the truest connection between you and your personal destiny. The Sacral Chakra encourages you to live life to the fullest. It moves you to do the things that you love and to be the person you truly aspire to be. A life without passion is almost pointless. Without passion, we are life's passive subjects. However, when the Sacral Chakra bolsters our desires, we become active participants in the world.

PLEASURE

Pleasure is, without a doubt, one of life's greatest motivations. The Sacral Chakra focuses on satisfying immediate pleasures, such as sexual impulses, and travelling down the longer road of personal destiny. Work and play flow through this chakra, making it possible to pursue a joyful life, filled with feelings of completeness – within yourself and when you're with your lover, your family, and the rest of the universe – rather than a mechanical life that feels like a chore.

DESIRE or AVERSION

To cultivate feelings of wholeness or harmony with the universe, desire must already exist. Desire is the strong feeling that what you want is what you need. To get what you need, you must first want it, and then you must act with intention. The Sacral Chakra fine-tunes desire until it becomes a strong tool for accomplishment. Without desire, there is aversion - and aversion is a product of fear. With desire, you are ready to grab life by its horns. Without it, you are likely to deny all that life offers. The Sacral Chakra prepares us to embrace life in all its many forms and accept our role in the world wholeheartedly.

History shows us that, for most of our existence on this planet, humans have been very community-oriented. Over time, as society slowly moved away from an exclusively tribal way of life, our individual sense of self solidified. We developed our own bodily awareness, and we learned to establish our individual needs, wants, and boundaries. This also occurs as we move from childhood into adolescence and we begin to move away from our "tribe" (family) to discover our own self.

In the line of ascending chakras, the Sacral is one up from the Root. The Root Chakra connects us with the Earth, our tribe or community, and our sense of survival. When it is balanced, we trust the Earth's capacity to provide all that we need to survive. Now, when we move to the Sacral Chakra, we begin to connect with our sense of self and everything we can achieve. We begin to come up with evolved, original, and creative ideas to satisfy those basic needs - and we begin to have fun!

The Way We Conceive Determines The Outcome

As we pointed out, the Sacral Chakra is closely related to our conception and gestation, and how we were created or conceived can impact how we later create or conceive our life projects.

In this sense, if your conception was accidental, then you may conceive your projects "accidentally," without giving much thought to their consequences. If you were conceived in a violent act, then it is possible that every time you begin to create a new life project, you may feel as if you have to fight all the way through it. On the other hand, if you were conceived in an act of love, commitment, and dedication, then you will probably conceive your projects in the same manner, with a deep appreciation and inner power.

It is important to note here that this will be the case unless other events or situations (in your upbringing, for example) have helped create patterns or belief systems opposed to the original ones.

How is this useful? When we are aware of the energy that prevails in us from our conception and we don't like how our lives are shaping up, we have the option to do things differently. We can choose to give ourselves the opportunity to create and develop our projects in life from the energy of love and passion. We can let go of thoughts such as: "Everything always goes wrong for me," "Why do I always get the opposite of what I want?" and "I don't know what I'm doing here."

Many will argue – and with good reason! – that it's impossible to remember the moment of our conception. However, we can pay attention to stories we overhear from our parents or close relatives regarding the situation surrounding the moment of our birth and what was happening around the time when our mothers became pregnant with us. We can also just observe how we tend to begin things in life, and I assure you that, if you examine your own behavior, you will find clues as to how you were conceived. You can also try the visualization exercise that I explain later in this book.

It's important to understand that we always go through the phases of conception, gestation, and birth in everything concerning our lives and projects. Therefore, it is vital to heal our conception, if it was not carried out in a conscious or loving way, in order for us to begin cultivating fresh new realities in our lives.

I will now offer an example in order to clarify how we can conceive thoughts and emotions as conscious beings, with the goal of creating realities that benefit our well-being. Always remember that, depending on the nature of how you conceive your thoughts and emotions, you will attract a variety of people and situations to your life. You create according to your emotionalized thoughts. If your thoughts and ideas are conceived from trust and worthiness and aligned with your inner power- good for you!

If, on the other hand, you conceive your project from a sense of struggle and scarcity, this is the energy that will dominate what you attract. It's the energy that will be present in the development (or "gestation") of your project and, ultimately, in its outcome (or "birth"). However, the wonderful part is that we always have a choice and an opportunity to do things differently, to re-create our lives in order to establish better outcomes.

How Can You Tell If Your Sacral Chakra Is Imbalanced?

Emotional balance is the essence of the Sacral Chakra. It's all about being fluid and flexible in our relationships with others, the world, and all our worldly attachments. At the core of our emotional being is the ability to adapt to constantly changing feelings and subtle energies. With this emotional fluidity come creativity and our ability to express ourselves uniquely and sincerely. A balanced Sacral Chakra is open and receptive to the flux of energies, with clearly defined and respectable boundaries.

So, how can you tell if your Sacral Chakra is imbalanced? When the Sacral Chakra is unstable, our emotional and physical bodies become disturbed. An imbalance can manifest in the form of an emotionless existence or by becoming too sensitive to all the drama in the world. A person with an imbalanced Sacral Chakra can be distant, apathetic, and complacent, or become compulsive, ruled by sporadic emotions, and susceptible to setback and defeat. Between these extremes, the specific way an imbalance manifests will depend on our personal belief system and how we tend to react to certain life situations.

Emotional and Mental States of an Imbalanced Sacral Chakra

1. You feel something is "wrong" with you.

Since the Sacral Chakra is the dwelling place of your conscious self, an imbalance could result in a lack of confidence and insecurity. You might feel uncomfortable in your own body or with your sexuality. The chakra's imbalance might leave you feeling vulnerable, confused and unfamiliar to yourself. You might be unable to connect sincerely with others.

2. You're out of touch with your feelings.

The Sacral Chakra is the seat of our emotions and feelings. Because emotions are susceptible to outside influence, it may be hard to understand what's happening and why. Perhaps you are typically empathetic and caring toward others but lately you find yourself devoid of compassion. Or, you could be a very level-headed person, but suddenly realize that your emotions have been overly dramatic. Unless your chakra is well-balanced, unruly waves in the sea of emotions could leave you an emotional wreck.

3. You're resistant to change.

The Sacral Chakra stabilizes your own emotions and feelings. A resistance to change comes from an inability to "flow" with changing relationships or life situations. When there's an inblance here, "going with the flow" seems like a challenge. When the Sacral Chakra is in tune with your body and with the universe, however, it helps you recognize that change is a necessary part of life, inevitable for personal growth. Resistance to change stems from emotional insecurity and indicates an inability to adjust to the constant ebb and flow of life.

4. You practice excessively controlling behavior.

Having a compulsive desire to control every aspect of life can be a sign of a seriously imbalanced Sacral Chakra. This is especially true when the drive extends into the unrealistic, like trying to control another person's life or obsessing over the arbitrary. This excessive attitude spells out one clear thing: you are afraid of life. Once the Sacral Chakra is balanced, you will love life and have no trouble releasing the illusion of control and accepting the harmony that is inherent in the universe.

5. You experience a lack of joy.

The Sacral Chakra houses many of our hedonistic and positive emotions, such as pleasure and joy. If there is an obvious lack of joy, there are possibly other suppressed emotions bottled and bubbling beneath the surface. These internalized emotions - whether they be fear, anger, guilt, jealousy, or shame - need to be acknowledged, expressed, and released in order for true joy to come forth. If left unchecked, emotional disturbance can manifest as a physical disease.

Negative or melancholic patterns are also easy to develop. These patterns soon turn into habits. You should ask yourself: "How often do I do things that make me truly happy? How often do I do things that make me unhappy?"

6. You have difficulty thinking outside the box.

The flow of creativity and original thought comes effortlessly when the Sacral Chakra is in harmony. You are naturally creative and imaginative. If there are difficulties within the creation process, the reason might be a lack of passion. You might feel like you are sleepwalking through your daily routine and everything is drab, gray, and stale. Stuck emotions, such as long-standing grief, or a traumatizing past event that still holds painful feelings, could also be the reason you can't break out of the dull cycle.

7. You're overly empathetic.

The Sacral Chakra establishes boundaries and houses your emotions. When this chakra is not in harmony, you may experience an emotional feeling akin to having left the gates left wide open: you are susceptible to anything that comes in and out. You might pick up too easily on other people's emotions or discomforts and adopt them as your own. Conversely, you could end up smothering people with your own emotions as you try to help. Soon, your sense of empathy can become completely whacked, leaving you utterly exhausted.

8. You're a workaholic.

Being overly attached to things you routinely do or create is a sign that the Sacral Chakra may be out of harmony. You might be addicted or compulsive when it comes to your work, material possessions, friends, family, or home. You have trouble stepping back from long stretches of tedious office tasks or taking a simple break. If you are skilled in a craft, you might catch yourself repeating the same things consistently without giving them much thought. The balanced Sacral Chakra knows how to harmonize work and play to create an orchestra, effectively enriching our quality of life.

9. You have difficulty enjoying sexuality.

The pleasure-seeking Sacral Chakra governs our primal urges, including our sexual impulses. When it's imbalanced, you might have trouble expressing yourself in an intimate relationship, have issues obtaining a relationship, or you may not have the slightest interest in sensuality. On the other end of the spectrum, you may give yourself too freely without connection to genuine feelings.

10. You lack creativity.

The Sacral Chakra is a creative force. It harbors the essence of your personality and hosts the artist in yourself. However, if the Sacral Chakra is askew, inspiration for creation might be scant, motivation null, and desire void. You may lack any imagination whatsoever. The Sacral Chakra is sexual by nature - as well as creative, playful, and imaginative - in order to resonate with and attract love.

Physical Symptoms of an Imbalanced Sacral Chakra

This chakra is located in the center of the lower naval, and it governs the lower back, joints, digestion, sexual organs, urinary tract, and kidneys.

1. Sexual Dysfunction

This category encompasses many hormonal problems dealing with fertility and the sexual organs. Infertility, irregular menstrual cycles, miscarriages, low libido, impotence, premature ejaculation, pre-menstrual syndrome, and pre-menstrual dysphoric disorder can all be affected by an imbalanced Sacral Chakra. Other related dysfunctions include uterine fibroids, poly ovarian cyst syndrome, and prostate problems.

2. Urinary Tract Disorders

These are mainly urinary tract infections, kidney stones, and bladder problems.

3. Lower Digestive Tract Disorders

These exist mainly through the small and large intestines. You may experience excessive gas, accompanied by either constipation or diarrhea, and other disorders such as IBS.

4. Lower Back Afflictions, Sciatica, Arthritis or Stiff Joints

When ignored, a buildup of negative thoughts or emotions won't dissipate. However, it may find other places within the body to manifest in less than desirable ways. It could lead to chronic discomfort, sharp, stabbing cramps in the lower back, shooting nerve pain, inflammation, or sore joints.

5. Sexually Transmitted Diseases and Infections.

These include the whole arena of sexually transmitted medical issues - AIDS, HIV, herpes, yeast infections, syphilis, human pappilomavirus, gonorrhea, and so on.

These physical and emotional states are clearly intertwined with the harmonious function of the Sacral Chakra. Since a physical disease often feeds on mental and emotional states, it's always best to begin healing the emotional self before the physical. So, when treating any of these afflictions, it's always necessary to energetically balance your chakras using Reiki, meditation, visualization, positive affirmations, or other techniques. It's important to seek balance because the chakras nourish us with a direct flow of life and healing energy.

What Can Cause Your Sacral Chakra to Become Imbalanced?

As the center of our emotions, it's easy for the Sacral Chakra to spin out of balance. We are, after all, emotional beings. We love, laugh, create, procreate, and feel sheer joy by simply being alive. We also sometimes express hatred, engage in destructive actions, and become deeply depressed.

Through infancy, childhood, and most of our adulthood, we learn ways to hide our emotions, stifle feelings we believe are unacceptable, and keep our rational selves in control of our lives. We often give up creative expression, sacrificing it in favor of material pursuits. We may spend our energy in trying to please others, to be what they want us to be, rather than risk being who we are inside. We become our own worst enemy.

A certain amount of negative feelings is a normal part of life. But when negativity rules over everything, it's time to take a closer look at what the Sacral Chakra is storing and what has led to the harmful emotional stores that have affected our ability to live in balance and at peace with ourselves.

Childhood trauma that left us emotionally disconnected

A fortunate few of us are raised in loving and supportive environments where we are allowed to grow into emotionally healthy adults. The rest of us face myriad struggles, often continuing into an adulthood in which we are out of harmony with who we really are. This can significantly impact our power to lead happy and healthy lives.

Being told you were an unwanted baby

Sometimes our struggles start before or immediately after birth when, for one reason or another, we're brought forth as an unwanted baby. How we're treated can convey unworthiness, but some mothers fighting their own battles also make it clear, verbally, that we are unloved. We might have been told what a burden we are or how we've ruined someone's life by our mere existence. Or perhaps we're shunted aside in favor of a sibling. Because of our childhood dependence on adults, we attempt to mold ourselves into being what they want us to be, rather than being who we were meant to be. The more we succeed at changing ourselves to satisfy others, the greater our betrayal of our essence.

Raised in an environment where emotions could not be expressed

Children are often subjected to emotional traumas, even by well-meaning parents. Love may be withheld for minor transgressions. We may be taught that it's wrong to express ourselves, especially emotionally. For example, we're told that "big kids don't cry," or to "control ourselves," and suppress our pain. We must, of course, learn what appropriate behavior is, but sometimes the lines are drawn too rigidly between what's acceptable and what isn't. The freedom to express ourselves is buried, sometimes so deeply that it may never return.

Overly strict upbringing with too many rules, repressing pleasure and enjoyment

We are frequently taught to fear. Sometimes fear is necessary for our safety, such as fear of getting burned if we stick our hands in a fire. But some of us learn to fear as a way of life. We may be physically beaten if we break the rules. We learn to be afraid of saying what we feel, knowing we'll be ridiculed if we do. We continue to hide our thoughts and feelings as adults, fearing we'll lose our jobs or jeopardize our relationships if we decide to be creative and break the rules and try a new idea. We lose our confidence, our happiness, and our self-respect, because we are untrue to ourselves.

Few outlets for creativity

Some rules are necessary for our protection, but others serve to stifle our creativity. Many of us simply aren't allowed to enjoy the delight that comes from just being a kid, exploring the world around us and our place in it. Experimentation is discouraged, closing off our creative channels. We have to color inside the lines, always making the sky blue and the trees green. We aren't allowed to use our blocks to build the house we see in our minds. The stories we write must be logical, with the characters behaving in reasonable ways. We must follow established pathways and not long for the roads untaken. Then when we become frustrated or resentful when our thirst for creativity isn't acknowledged, we are told to go to our rooms and watch TV or given some mindless chore to complete. Over time, we "forget" how to create and bury our originality in daily minutiae.

Overemphasis on pleasurable stimulation

The opposite of a too-restrictive environment is one in which adults engage in constant entertainment and partying. Although it may be pleasurable stimulation, as children we can become overstimulated, developing our own perceived need for continuous action. As we grow up, this need may give rise to round after round of frenzied activity or, even worse, to drug or alcohol abuse or other equally destructive behavior. In either case, we ignore the more tranquil aspects of our personalities and are untrue to ourselves.

Raised in an environment that repressed joy and pleasure

Many of us are taught to repress joy and pleasure, learning that the world around us is a dark place where we must be concerned with important matters in order to survive. Play turns into work, rather the other way around. We are discouraged, sometimes even punished, for what are deemed trivial activities. Success at any cost is a common mantra, with no allowance for having fun until "later." Unless we make a concerted effort as adults, later never comes. We keep our noses to the grindstone, spending our lives in careers or relationships we often dislike to avoid being accused of not taking life seriously or being thought of as frivolous. Any delight in life is stifled in the false belief that what gives us pleasure is wrong, resulting in an imbalance in emotional health.

Growing up feeling ashamed about one's sexuality

Sex is the one area in which nearly all of us feel imbalanced in one way or another. Childhood sexual abuse is the worst kind of sexual trauma - one that can literally destroy an individual. Because children are usually at the mercy of the adult abusers, they learn to shut themselves off from feeling, to literally disconnect from their emotions. Lives can become terribly distorted, regardless of how little or often the abuse occurs. These children may reach maturity as cold, emotionless adults, or, on the opposite end of the spectrum, become sexually promiscuous. Either lifestyle is destructive mentally, emotionally, and physically. Even with therapy, the ability to have pleasurable sex is often elusive.

Although not a trauma, growing up believing that sexuality is shameful can lead to an inability to accept the natural part of us that enjoys sex. We may learn that touching ourselves is bad or that our bodies are ugly. We may be teased about the ways our body changes as we go through puberty. We can become self-conscious, embarrassed, or ashamed. Later, we may experience difficulty in achieving healthy intimacy with our sexual partner. We may engage in meaningless sex with multiple partners or act out our repressed sexual energy in other inappropriate or harmful ways.

The lack of emotional harmony in our lives results in an inability to trust our own instincts - our gut feelings - about what is right and what is wrong for us. The inability to be our natural selves and express our true emotions, the betrayals of who we are, and the denials of how we really feel are all stored in the Sacral Chakra, depleting our energy, weakening our life force, and creating an imbalance that keeps us from achieving the health and happiness we deserve.

Five Common Questions Related to the Sacral Chakra

Since the Sacral Chakra handles many aspects of a gratifying life, including sex, pleasure, relationships, joy, emotions, and creativity, many people want to know more about balancing this powerful area of their energetic system.

Below are five questions often asked about the Sacral Chakra:

1. I have heard that both the Second Chakra (Sacral) and the Fifth Chakra (Throat) are related to creativity. What's the difference?

Yes! Both the Sacral and Throat Chakras have a special and yet very different relationship with creativity.

The Sacral Chakra represents many important aspects of your personal power and emotional issues. It is the major hub for creativity. The Sacral Chakra is like a key that unlocks the door of your creative potential. Because this Chakra is located below the belly button or womb, it is considered the birthing place for ideas, inspirations, and the ability to express oneself freely.

The Fifth Chakra or Throat Chakra also contributes to our creativity, but in a different way. It is the center for communication, which involves creative expression through speech or writing.

When the Sacral Chakra gives birth to your creative ideas, this energy bursts forth and flows freely to provide the energy you use to create. Emotional artistic endeavors - such as dance, art, or movement - that are representative of your sexual self are also expressed here.

The Fifth Chakra takes those inspirational energies and transforms them into creative thoughts and actions. From there, creativity can be released in the form of your choosing. Your Throat Chakra expresses creativity outwardly in perhaps a more communicative process. Writing, music, public speaking, and many other creative pursuits that involve the projection of ideas are products of a balanced Throat Chakra.

Consider this concept. Have you ever experienced a time when you were bursting with energy and an urge to be creative? It was as if you were completely driven by a deep fire compelling you to create – otherwise, you felt as if you might explode. Your Sacral Chakra is behind those creative energies. Did you produce something wonderful or were you stifled somehow and unable to follow through on your project? This is where your Throat Chakra plays a vital role in transforming that energy into form.

Since the Sacral Chakra is the Second Chakra, it involves the "lower" aspects of the self, while the Fifth Chakra has more dealings with one's "higher" self.

All in all, any creativity must be processed through both Chakras in order to become something tangible. If one or both are blocked, it will be difficult to follow through on any of our creative desires. Open and balanced Second and Fifth Chakras, however, will lend themselves to a highly creative, open life, filled with abundance and a generous flow of inspiration.

2. Can I balance my own Sacral Chakra or do I need to work with a professional?

You can absolutely balance your own Sacral Chakra! If you find yourself having troubles in areas controlled by the Second Chakra, simply being aware of them is the first step in transforming these energies.

Below are a few easy ways to clear your Sacral Chakra (more techniques explained in later chapters):

- Dance: That's right - shake, spin, twirl, and move those hips like no one is watching. Belly dancing is an especially useful method to open the Sacral Chakra. Dancing in general is a wonderful way to open those energetic channels and invigorate your sexual, emotional, and self-energies.

- Affirmations: If you're struggling with this Chakra, a great affirmation can go a long way in helping you focus on clearing. Repeat: "I am vital and passionate. I am healthy. I am myself. I am confident and achieving my dreams."

- Orange you glad? Orange is the color that represents the Sacral Chakra. It's an energetic color so try visualizing it. Imagine a glowing orange ball nestled inside your lower abdomen, filling and warming you with powerful, comforting light.

- Balance: When working on one chakra, it's always good to check in with the other chakras as well. When one is out of whack, you can bet others may also require your attention. The chakras work together as a system, so using the ideas, techniques, and exercises in this book will help you to heal one area and balance the others, too! Additionally, you can use my audio meditation to balance all your chakras (you can find it on Amazon or iTunes - or get it Free when you buy my book, *The Root Chakra*).

- Yoga - There are many terrific Yoga poses and stretches designed to open the Sacral Chakra. These techniques will not only energize you, they'll have a wonderful effect on your body. You'll see which poses are perfect for balancing your Sacral Chakra later on in this book.

Cooking - The Sacral Chakra loves experiencing food, and cooking is a fun way to enhance our creative juices and literally savor the moment.

If you find yourself having difficulty clearing your own Chakra, you can always reach out to an expert in energetic healing. You can also simply try talking to a friend or loved one. Often just sharing with another person helps release any problematic or blocked energy to which you've been subconsciously clinging. A professional can also help with energy movement and, moreover, healing blockages. The goal is to do what you need to do to feel safe, open, and balanced.

3. How can my partner and I work on our Sacral Chakra to improve our sex lives?

The Sacral Chakra does deal with our sexual organs, flow, and sexual satisfaction. It's also the hub for passion and experiencing pleasure. Often blockages here are related to feelings of shame, guilt, and negative sexual stereotypes.

In order to enjoy a passionate and open sexual partnership, both you and your partner should take a look to see whether you've been hoarding any emotional baggage. Often there are past issues that can greatly impact how we view ourselves and how we relate to the opposite sex. A searching self-inventory is especially important if there has ever been a negative past experience, such as sexual or emotional abuse, rape, or if there is any extreme religious guilt present. All of these concerns should be addressed in a loving, trusting environment with your partner.

You can do this by planning to sit down together at a time when neither of you are facing any interruptions or distractions. Make sure both of you are aware that you've set aside this time specifically for opening your chakras and learning about each other's inner workings. This may take some time and you may prefer to simply address one area of your sexual and emotional self at a time. The pace is entirely up to you.

Together, discuss some of these intimate questions.

- How do you feel about sex?
- How were you raised to feel about sex? Do these experiences affect you now?
- Do you have any guilt or shame associated with sexual experiences or pleasure?
- Do you feel deserving of love?
- Are you comfortable receiving love?
- Are you able to show love?
- Is there anything that makes you feel uncomfortable or scared?

Communication acts as a wonderful initial tool for creating healthy, flowing Sacral Chakras. Together, as you learn to release any past emotional blocks, traumas, or outdated belief systems, you can begin to explore the depths of your sexual intimacy.

You and your partner can also have a lot of fun by letting go, being in the moment, and enjoying pleasure – together! Playfulness, affection and touch are also ways to open your Second Chakra. Here are some great ideas for couples:

- Try a massage – touch is always good for the Sacral Chakra.
- Dance! Dancing is sexually stimulating and helps our body communicate sexual energy.
- Share fantasies – try something new.
- Laugh together.
- Tickle one another.
- When it's time to get frisky, keep the lights on.
- Explore the art of Tantric Sex.

- Write love letters.

- Play the word game – the giver spells something on the receiver's back and the receiver tries to guess the word!

When you work on Sacral Chakras as a couple, your goal is to find trust in one another and create the bond of intimacy your Second Chakra was designed to promote. When two people are completely open and trusting, the sexual experience will be beautiful, spiritual, and completely satisfying. This can take time to develop and perfect. Try not to have expectations of yourself or project any expectations onto yourself as to what you think your partner may want. Ultimately, the best sexual experiences are the ones in which both individuals are completely in the moment and focused on sensory pleasures and emotional connection.

4. Can an imbalance in the Sacral Chakra affect what I eat?

This is a common question and the answer is a definite yes! For the Second Chakra, food represents pleasure. It isn't just about nutrition; it's about the experience! You want to enjoy the texture, the feel, the smell, the flavor, and the creation of your cuisine.

When this Chakra is out of balance, you may find yourself overindulging or having unhealthy cravings. This is the body's way of telling you that you are depleted or hungry for something else.

Have you ever experienced an instance when you just couldn't stop eating, even though you weren't physically hungry? Perhaps your body was telling you to stop, but the temptation to continue overwhelmed you. These are signs your Sacral Chakra is out of balance.

If this Chakra is imbalanced, we may experience irresistible cravings for starches, such as pasta, bread or wheat, chocolate and sweets, or high-fat foods. Often these relate to either a need to hide our bodies, perhaps stemming from weight and obesity issues, or our need to be touched or soothed. The latter is why we may crave sugary foods or chocolate, which relate to our sexual center. When consumed in abundance, starchy or high-fat foods relate to a desire to cover up shame by providing the body with temporary fullness and comfort. Since the Sacral Chakra also assists with the flow of our personal energy, it's also possible to experience cravings related to substances that overstimulate us, like an excess of caffeine, refined sugars or even drug abuse.

This is not to say that, when your Second Chakra is balanced, you will never experience any cravings. Treating yourself to occasional pleasures loved by your Second Chakra is different than experiencing constant cravings and participating in unhealthy indulgences. If you are eating too much, your Sacral Chakra is hinting at unfulfillment somewhere in your emotional self. Determining the roots of this unfulfillment will help you realign yourself both physically and emotionally. If you can pinpoint the root of your emptiness, intense food cravings will diminish and your body will readjust.

5. How do I know when my Sacral Chakra is open and balanced?

Your Sacral Chakra is balanced when you feel one with yourself, your identity, your sexuality, and your ability to enjoy life fully and passionately. You are in-balance when your life feels joyful, creative, and pleasurable. You will feel a connection with others and others will be attracted to your positive energy. Sexual experiences will be pleasurable, without shame or guilt. Your Sacral Chakra plays a vital role in moving energy from your lower to your higher self. Opening this gateway will help promote creativity and allow your other chakras to manifest your needs.

A healthy Sacral Chakra allows you to live in the moment. Your sense of self and your confidence become so strong that you attract plenty of opportunities and experience life to its fullest! Maintaining a balanced Sacral Chakra is of utmost importance. Its connection to the other chakras will help create incredible channels of energy - both creative and sensual - allowing you to be who you were always meant to be!

If you are free from reproductive problems and strong in your lower back, you may have a healthy Second Chakra.

If your digestion is good, you have no overwhelming cravings in your diet, and you enjoy a healthy sex life, chances are your Sacral Chakra is functioning normally.

If you enjoy your life and other people aren't upset by life's ups and downs, and don't feel the need to prove yourself, you may be sure that your Second Chakra is in order.

Physical pain often illustrates a deeper truth about our lives. Emotional issues have a tendency to remain not just in our psyches, but also in our tissues. These tissues - including sites of previous trauma and various organs - are each related to a specific chakra. These damaged tissues often remain, at some level, in the body. If these are not dealt with on a conscious level, they can cause failures in our structural or organ systems.

Clearing emotional pain is the premier path to joy, both in the body and in our relation to others and the world. Exercises designed to turn these conditions around (look elsewhere in this book for more specific examples) may seem simple, but their effects can be profound. Change may come slowly, but take time to appreciate your efforts and have faith that the outcome will be worth the wait.

PART II – BALANCE YOUR SACRAL CHAKRA

Balance Your Sacral Chakra with these Simple Techniques

Technique #1: Visualizing Your Conception

This visualization is meant to connect you with the moment of your conception, enabling you to relate to how you currently conceive your life projects. From there, you can decide whether you need to do things differently in order to achieve a fuller life.

You can record this exercise in your own voice and then listen to it while you visualize.

Find a quiet place where you will not be interrupted. Remember to put your phone on silent mode. If you want, you can put some meditation music on to help you to get into a meditative state.

Lie down someplace other than a bed so you won't easily fall asleep. You want to be relaxed but awake.

To begin, get in a very relaxed position, keeping your spine straight.

Now close your eyes and take three deep breaths. Become aware of your breathing. Focus your attention on the air as you inhale and exhale. Notice how the rhythm of your breathing becomes slower, deeper, more serene, effortless.

Feel the air flowing through your body. Notice as it moves in and out through your nose, taking all the worries and tensions from your body. Breathe.

Bring your attention to your feet and imagine an energizing, healing light coming through the soles of your feet. It moves up to your ankles, then your thighs, and as it travels through your body it eliminates any fears about the future, any fears about your next steps. In this way you're entering a deep state of relaxation.

Now imagine that the light is travelling up, toward your hips, your intestines, and your reproductive system, healing and revitalizing each of these areas as it moves through them. You are increasingly serene as you enter a deep state of relaxation.

Now that light moves up and fills your stomach area and then your chest, healing and revitalizing your organs. It moves up into your upper back and penetrates each vertebra of your spine, eliminating the burdens of the past.

That warm, healing light continues up to your shoulders and then down your arms to your hands, removing all fear of love and being loved.

Finally, you feel the light move up and over your neck, head, scalp, forehead, eyes, cheeks, and lips, relaxing you more and more.

When the body is completely relaxed, the mind quiets and you feel your whole body.

Now visualize yourself as a being made of light, a divine being of light and love floating through the Universe. Imagine that you're free from the barriers of time and space. Breathe.

Now it's time to choose a physical form -it's the moment of your conception.

You're searching the Universe´s vast possibilities in order to find those ideal circumstances that offer what you want to experience in life - the people, places, and things that will surround you, giving you the experiences that will help you learn what you need to know and teach others what you came to share.

You look around and choose the planet for your birth - you choose planet Earth. Think about that choice. Why did you choose Earth? Pay attention to your thoughts: "The reason why I chose to come to Earth is...."

Consider the first thoughts and emotions that pop into your head and heart. Observe yourself choosing where and how you will take physical form.

> What country are you born into?

> What city do you live in?

> What race are you?

> Which religion have you chosen?

> Who is your mother?

> Who is your father?

Answer the following:

> The reason I chose my mother was....

> The reason I chose my father was....

Examine your thoughts, emotions, and feelings. They are all important clues in understanding what you are here to learn and to teach!

Continue observing:

> Do you have siblings?

> What is your economic status?

> Who are your grandparents?

> Are there any diseases in your family?

> What is going on in the world at the time of your conception?

> What's going on in the country?

> Is there peace? War? Any kind of crisis?

Now you have reached the very moment of your conception. You already selected all the circumstances for your manifestation into physical form.

Visualize yourself as you prepare for conception.

You see your parents at the time of your conception. What is dad thinking as he makes love to mom? What is dad feeling as he makes love to mom? Breathe; observe your thoughts, emotions, and sensations.

Now consider what mom is thinking as she makes love to dad. What is mom feeling as she makes love to dad? Stay in the moment, keep breathing, and pay attention to your thoughts, emotions, and sensations.

Your consciousness is transferred to your mother's womb. Pay attention to the first thoughts and emotions that occur to you here. Breathe deeply and complete these thoughts:

> The reason why I choose to be alive is....
>
> My mission in life is....

Breathe and pay close attention to your thoughts.

Finally, take three deep breaths and slowly move your legs and hands. Stretch and, when you're ready, open your eyes.

This exercise can be more or less uncomfortable, depending on the beliefs and emotions you relate to sex. The important thing is to observe everything you think and feel throughout the exercise. Doing so will give you important information about how you conceive your life projects, which has an important impact on the way you then develop your these projects.

You cannot change the circumstances of your conception, but you can understand that it was a choice made by your Higher Self in order to learn and then share those lessons. Once you become conscious of what's limiting your growth, you can say, "Lesson learned!" and turn the page to something better. Remember, you have the power to do everything differently now!

Technique #2: What Brings You Joy?

Often the word "joy" is confused with happiness or satisfaction. Happiness can be fleeting and dependent on external circumstances or environments relating to your physical well-being. Did you sleep well last night? Is the weather nice? Are you content with your partner? These moments of happiness tend to flow in and out, depending on what is happening around us. The same goes for satisfaction. A satisfying moment is one in which you feel like there's nothing more you could possibly need or want. Yet, neither happiness nor satisfaction are representations of the inner you - the joyful you.

The Sacral Chakra opens up and supports our ability to feel joy. It's something that many of us struggle to find and preserve, and, as a result, we seek outside influences to satisfy our needs and bring temporary happiness. Unlike happiness and satisfaction, joyfulness can be a lasting state of being. It comes only from within and provides a deep sense of connection to purpose, well-being, and self-acceptance.

The funny thing about joy is that it has to be fostered. It's a garden you must carefully tend, planting seeds of patience and cultivating blooms that represent what you truly want to do with your life. Properly cultivated, the garden will give you the opportunity to continuously grow, learn, evolve, and pay it forward.

The beauty of this is that, once you find your joy, there's no cap on how much you can have! When you learn to balance your ambitions and achievements, you will discover a harmony that resides within. You'll begin to find peace with your reality, no matter what challenges or changes arise.

At times, difficult experiences may make you feel clouded, affecting your ability to feel joy and accept life as it comes. Instead of seeking true joy, you're tempted to seek quick-fix moments of satisfaction that ultimately won't fulfill your inner desires.

Below you will find an exercise designed to help you remember what brings you joy.

First, grab a pen and piece of paper and jot down these very important questions. If you use a journal, you can use it to complete this exercise.

- What do you love?

- What inspires you?

- What activities make you lose track of time?

- What feels easy and natural to you?

- What gets you excited?

- What feels meaningful to you?

- What are you most passionate about?

It's important not to overthink this activity. For each question, simply write down the first answer that pops into your mind, even if what comes up seem absurd or unimportant. Don't judge yourself. Your logical mind may try and trick you, but trust your gut instincts and your Sacral Chakra. If you have trouble coming up with an answer, think back to when you were a child and consider what would have made your day back then.

Nobody knows you better than you know yourself, so only you can answer these questions truthfully. You can ask others for their insight, but you have the last word on what truly brings you joy.

Next, try this step-by-step method to help you further evaluate the joyfulness in your life.

1. Find a setting that inspires you, where you can sit and meditate on the things that give meaning to your life. This can be a place in nature or somewhere that makes you feel peaceful, safe, and secure. Be present and aware as the quiet voice within begins to talk. Ask yourself what you're passionate about. Allow yourself to daydream about the times in your life when you felt the happiest. Were you happiest as a child? Did you dance

or paint for hours with a pure, open heart, free from self-consciousness? Did you climb trees or dream beneath starlit skies? Did you go camping or draw or hike? Perhaps something you used to have in your life brought you great joy, like music, photography, scrapbooking, art, or writing. Whatever it was, simply thinking about it will give you a feeling of joy. Your heart will sing as you remember these moments of joy, because these were times when you were completely present. These were times when you weren't feeling regretful about the past or stressed over the future, but, rather, content in the moment.

2. Create a list of these joyful memories. Start with the ones that bring you the greatest joy. Once you've chosen your most joyful memory, think about what you need to do to relive that feeling and jot it down. If you used to happily sing all day, you don't need to quit your job to start studying music. Instead, cultivate joy by singing in the car on your way to work or while you take a bath or tidy up the house. Take part in a local choir or sing at your church.

3. Without blame, ask yourself what happened. What led you away from the path to joyfulness? What made you stop doing the things you loved to do? Write these reflections down. Then, put your hands over your heart and quietly forgive yourself. Let your heart fill with compassion. Be aware that you are not a victim and life is yours for the making. You can *choose* to do things that bring you joy.

You can *choose* to do things differently, starting now.

4. Finally, make a pact to experience joy as often as possible. Commit to doing more of the things that make you joyful. Whatever it is that you need to do to make this happen, do it! You don't need to invest a ton of time to allow some joy into your life. If it's all you can manage, start by setting aside a small amount of time for these activities. As little as fifteen minutes here and there will help you work joy back into your life. Your soul will be singing again in no time at all.

Reintroducing joy into your life should be nothing less than a commitment. Make joy a priority by scheduling joyfull sessions on your calendar or letting your loved ones in on your plans. Ultimately, you're giving yourself permission to live joyfully from now on.

Always remember to be gentle and patient with your self-growth. Don't be hard on yourself. Just as it takes years to create the habits of self-doubt and blame, it also takes time to clear the weeds and cultivate the gifts of joy. Begin planting seeds now and you'll soon find yourself enjoying a beautiful garden filled with every sense of joy and fulfilment you could ever want.

Technique #3: Change the Frequency to Dial into New Creations

This easy and powerful exercise aims to make us aware of how our behavior affects our lives. Remember that as we think and feel, we act. Our actions then create our reality. How do these creations manifest themselves? People, situations, and events that are perfectly aligned with the frequency of your thoughts and emotions will begin to make themselves known to you.

The hustle and bustle of our day-to-day lives takes us away from the here and now, and inadvertently we go from past to future missing the present moment. It is in the present moment where we become the consistent creator of our reality. However, we can be so distracted that we create based solely on past experiences and concerns for the future and, generally, these creations do not bring us optimal well-being.

In this sense, I suggest that, every few hours, you take a moment to stop what you're doing, take one to three deep breaths, and observe the kind of thoughts you're having in the moment. If these thoughts bring peace and harmony to your life, good for you! Keep up the good work! If, however, they worry and stress you out, you have the wonderful option to immediately change your thoughts and start feeling better.

To avoid creating a reality that vibrates at the same frequency of those negative thoughts, you must become aware of them and immediately cut them off. In their stead, think thoughts that connect you with your well-being. This is what I mean by "change your frequency."

Have you ever said, "I think I got up on the wrong side of the bed"? I'm sure you know what I mean: one day you wake up, burn your breakfast toast, and spill coffee on your shirt just as you're leaving for work. "Ugh! This day is already going wrong!" you say. It takes you a while to find the keys to your car, you get stuck in traffic, and then, when you get to work, nothing seems to go right. And so the day goes....

Sound familiar now? At times like this, it's important to remember that we always have a choice. We can become aware of what's happening to us and, if necessary, change our attitude. Even if you can't change what's going on in the moment, you can change how you feel about it. Remember this saying: "When we change the way we look at things, the things we look at change."

Going deeper into this exercise

At the end of the day, make yourself comfortable in a quiet spot and, if you want, play some relaxing music - preferably instrumental so you don't get distracted by lyrics. Close your eyes and take three deep breaths to release tension from your body. (You can use the meditation I gave you when you bought my book *The Root Chakra*.)

Next, think of an event in your life that made you feel uncomfortable. Observe whatever feelings manifest in your physical body. These may include chest palpitations, tightness around your throat, or a burning sensation in your stomach.

Direct all of your attention to the area where you're having a physical re-action. Simply observe without judgment and breathe. That's all you have to do - observe and breathe. Focus on the feeling, but don't cling to it – give it plenty of space. Keep breathing and observing until the sensations in your physical body slowly begin to diminish.

Repeat this exercise using a variety of unpleasant memories. Practice on a regular basis, and soon you'll be able to put a healthy amount of space between yourself, an unpleasant event, and the negative emotions it causes. You'll recognize that events like this no longer have any power over you, allowing you to release negative emotions, effectively creating more beneficial realities for yourself.

When you finish this exercise, go to your "sacred place," the place you go during meditation to find peace and recharge your energy. Be grateful for the opportunity to heal and finally open your eyes.

Now, go out and make your dreams come true!

Technique #4: Creating Your Perfect Day

In our exsistence in this particular dimension, emotions are inescapable. When our emotions are harmonious, we create harmonious realities. Of course, it's natural to sometimes feel negative emtoinos, like sadness, anger, and pain, and to fully live these emotions. It's not natural, however, to magnify those emotions and allow the ensuing drama to lead our lives. When we get lost in emotions and blow them out of proportion, we lose sight of the "now," running the risk of making bad or questionable decisions.

This simple exercise will help you get used to seeing yourself as a Creative Being and using the creative power of your Second Chakra to create new realities in your life.

Keep a notepad and a pen on your bedside table. When you wake up each morning, write down no more than three or four things that you want to accomplish that day. Start with simple goals. Remember to be specific and clear, for example:

- Today my drive to work will be peaceful; the traffic will be light.

- There's harmony in my home today.

- Time is on my side today; I have enough time to go to the gym.

- Today, I have the solution for [*X situation*] at work.

Mentally review your list several times a day and trust that you will accomplish what you set out to do that day. Do not stress out. Trust the energy that works with you and gives you guidance throughout the day, make sound decisions, take necessary actions, and stay alert to the signs that arise from your intuition.

At the end of the day, before bed, review your list and see how you did. What did you create in your day? Maybe you didn't succeed in achieving all three or four goals, but maybe you accomplished two. What a great start! Celebrate it! Recognize it as a proof of your power, because this is how you begin to tune into the energy of creation. Do this every day. Practice makes perfect!

Technique #5: Using Your Creative Power to Make Dreams Come True

In a new notepad, simply and clearly write down something you want. Next, write a phrase in which you give thanks for achieving or receiving the aforementioned item. Repeat this activity forty-nine times over the course of forty-nine days. Place your signature after each sentence, . This is another way to tune into a specific frequency to attract what you want.

If, for example, you reach day twenty-three and you forgot to do the exercise, you must start again from scratch. In other words, when you return to the exercise after a lapse, you must start again from day one.

When you've completed the exercise, gather all of your pages and burn them, giving thanks for what has been created and is coming your way. Always thank the Creative Source for all that you receive each day!

When you want to achieve something from the bottom of your heart, you're clear about what you want, have a burning desire to achieve it, and have unwavering faith that it will come to pass, the Universe will support you. You'll be placed within the necessary frequency to attract the people, events, and circumstances you need to make your dreams come true. Try it and you'll be amazed at the miracles you can attract into your life. I have witnessed this myself!

Here is an example:

I, Kelly, am thankful for my new car. Kelly S mith

I, Kelly, am thankful for my new car. Kelly S mith

I would like to remind you that if you feel any doubts or fears about having your dreams come true, you should first attend to those doubts, clearing them using the clearing technique of your choice. You are welcome to use the "Reduce Your Fears to Ashes" technique, which I explained in my book *Root Chakra*; it's a very effective way to free ourselves from beliefs that may be sabotaging our creative efforts.

More Techniques You Can Do on Your Own to Balance Your Sacral Chakra

A balanced Sacral Chakra is essential to help you enjoy life and all that it can bring you. Luckily, bringing this chakra back into balance is a fun process. The easiest ways to re-energize and heal your Second Chakra involve physical activities that enhance sacral circulation, positive affirmations, hand mudras to redirect your body's healing energies, sound therapy, nourishing foods, and other enjoyable exercises that you can practice easily on your own.

Physical Activities

Hula hip stretch (circular pelvic movements):

Like any other energy center in your body, your Sacral Chakra requires a good amount of healthy circulation to help clear out the stagnant, repressed energies and emotions that tend to get stuck there, including guilt, self-loathing, jealousy, and regret. While any kind of regular exercise is beneficial, you can enhance your regular workout by adding a hula-hoop to your repertoire. The circular pelvic motion used in this activity is perfect for loosening up the tension in your hips and lower back. If you can't get your hands on a hula-hoop, you can simulate its effect by putting your hands on your hips and pushing your hips all around in a big circle like you're moving an imaginary hula hoop in slow motion. Remember to practice rotating your hips equally in both directions to get a balanced flow going.

Kegel exercises (also great for the Root Chakra!)

Kegel exercises are excellent for both the Root and Sacral Chakras, and they strengthen all the muscles in the birth canal. Many women even report that Kegel exercises help enhance their sex lives, too. Simply put, a woman practices Kegel exercises by contracting and pulling up her vaginal muscles internally. A man can also practice a similar exercise by contracting the muscles of the perineum, directly in front of the anus, in order to help prevent premature ejaculations. A woman can check to see if she's been performing this exercise properly during a trip to the bathroom, simply by attempting to stop her urine midstream. The same muscles you use to stop your urine flow are the ones you contract during Kegel exercises. Because this exercise can be performed discreetly, you can practice your daily repetitions during your commute to work without anyone noticing!

Salsa, merengue, samba, and belly dancing

If you prefer dancing to the traditional workout routine, you can stimulate Sacral Chakra healing by learning, salsa, samba, meringue, or belly dancing. These dance styles help reawaken dormant sexual energy and give you feelings of confidence, empowering you to express yourself and your emotions.

Sensual Movement: Sex, strip tease, pole dancing

Of course, sex with a loving, respectful partner is also a positive way to unlock stagnant or repressed energy from your sacral center. Please note that if you are suffering from general fatigue, you should not overindulge in sexual relations, because doing so might weaken you even more; such people need to focus more on conserving and building up their energy reserves through the techniques described later in this chapter. You can also get in touch with your sensual side and activate your Sacral Chakra by moving sensually, performing a strip tease, or getting a little wild with some pole dancing. Remember to have fun with it! If you begin to feel uncomfortable, or these exercises exacerbate any negative beliefs regarding your sexuality, then these must be dealt with immediately in order to promote your healing.

Water activities

Given that water is the element associated with this chakra, any type of water activity, such as swimming, surfing, and water skiing can be an excellent way to balance this energy center.

Affirmations

There are times in our lives when we want to make changes in ourselves and give ourselves permission to "see ourselves," to ascertain what beliefs we hold to be true. Often, the beliefs that shape our lives don't truly come from within us. Instead, they were taken from our family, religion, friends, culture, or generational norms. Such beliefs might be etched in our memories since before we can even remember.

Then comes a time in our lives during which we recognize that we want to create a different reality for ourselves than the one we live in now. We recognize that our way of acting, thinking, and being have expired and won't allow us to evolve.

Making affirmations can help us during this process. When we take an honest self-inventory and discard limiting beliefs, it's as if we're removing layers, creating open space. How will we fill that space? That will depend on us, on what we want and need to create for our desired futures. Affirmations are an excellent way to create new programs in our subconscious to give us well-being, peace, and personal development.

Affirmations are short sentences with clear, strong messages that connect you with your Higher Self. To make affirmations work for us, we must first think of a short, clear sentence that describes how we wish to grow and move forward, and then we write it down, over and over, in a notebook. Write each sentence on its own line.

Take a sheet of paper, place it horizontally and divide it into two columns. In the left column, make your first affirmation, starting with "I, [your first name]."

The second column is called known as the response column. Here you will write the first thought or thoughts that come to mind as you write and mentally repeat the affirmation. In this way, you'll begin to connect with your subconscious programming and the beliefs that affect your daily life. The response column will be the key to the exercise, because it's there where you will begin to recognize the negative thinking that has been interfering with your growth.

Here is an example:

Affirmation

> *I, Laura, am a money magnet.*
>
> *I, Laura, am a money magnet.*
>
> *I, Laura, am a money magnet.*

Response Column

A money magnet? Really? I don´t even have a job.

Will this exercise work? It's boring. I'm sure no good will of this.

Even if I do get any money from doing this, I'm sure I'll lose it right away. Money never seems to stick to me.

Write the affirmation twenty times a day for fifteen consecutive days.

What if for some reason you couldn't do the exercise on day eight? You'd have to start again the next day as if you were on day one again. It's important to do this exercise every day - it won't take much time. And remember, this is an important exercise for you. It's not homework like when you were in school; it is a gift you are giving to yourself to help bring about the change you seek.

After fifteen days, burn these papers. Why should you do that? Because burning them will be an act of deep purification. You'll be burning all the negative energy that showed up in the response column. As the papers go up in flames, you will purify your personal energy.

Affirmation invites us to make a paradigm shift. The role of the response column is to help us extract any thoughts and feelings that were repressed and, in the end, to let go of them in a healthy manner. Therefore, make sure you write down everything that goes through your mind. When you're done, read it over and familiarize yourself with what's going on in your head. As you write, you're letting your beliefs out, perhaps without even realizing it.

What if I don't think of anything to write in the Response Column?

It doesn't matter. Write: "I can't think of anything." Don't be discouraged. As you continue the exercise, more and more thoughts will make themselves known.

What if good beliefs come out? Will I eliminate them when I burn the papers?

No. You can't eliminate the Truth of your Higher Self. These truths are only connected to that higher energy. Those thoughts and emotions that vibrate on a higher plane are part of your True Self and cannot be eliminated.

What time of the day is best for working on the affirmations?

Ideally, you should do this exercise at the beginning of your day or before going to bed. But the important thing is that you make them, no matter when! Keep your affirmations at the forefront of your mind as you go through your daily life, and continue to observe your own behavior. Be alert to changes when they begin to happen!

I will now leave you some statements that work well with the Sacral Chakra:

> *I, (your first name), am the woman/man I want to be.*
>
> *Since I, (your first name), choose to be here, I can be/do/have whatever I want.*
>
> *I, (your first name), can enjoy sex in the way that I choose.*
>
> *I, (your first name), open myself to receiving pleasure.*
>
> *I, (your first name), create my own experiences.*
>
> *I, (your first name), flow with life.*
>
> *I, (your first name), conceive brilliant ideas easily.*

Mudras

A *Mudra*, which is Sanskrit for "closure" or "seal," is a certain body position - mostly involving our hands and fingers - that influences the body's energy.

Mudras are great for conserving and balancing a weak Second Chakra. Based on ancient practices that go back thousands of years, Mudras are simple hand gestures that help channel the energy flow through the meridians of your body to promote healing and inner balance.

The following are some Mudras that you can use to balance your Sacral Chakra. They are particularly effective when you perform them during meditation, maintaining each hand position for at least fifteen minutes, preferably using both hands.

Yoni Mudra

There are several variations of the Yoni Mudra, but you can perform the basic one by putting your hands together with only the fingertips touching. From there, turn your hands so that your index fingers are pointing down toward the ground. Push your thumbs up toward your head. It will look like you have an almond shape in the space left between your hands. Rest your hands on your abdomen, just below your belly button, and start by holding this gesture for three minutes.

A variation of this Mudra can be seen in the following photo.

Yoni mudra
Seal of the inner source

Dhyani Mudra

The sacral center also benefits greatly from practicing the Dhyani Mudra. Perform the basic Dhyani Mudra by resting the back of your right hand inside the palm of the left hand so that the fingertips of your left hand touch the knuckles of your right hand. As you sit, rest your hands in this position in the center of your lap. Complete this Mudra by putting the tips of your thumbs together and lifting them so that both thumbs point up to your navel. This is an excellent Mudra to hold during meditation; it symbolizes the act of transcending the world of appearances in order to see the true nature of reality.

Dhyani mudra
Gesture of meditation
and contemplation

As you practice, increase the amount of time you hold these Mudras gradually by a few minutes each week. If you have any questions about your Mudra practice, don't hesitate to seek guidance from an experienced yoga teacher or energy healer.

Mantras and Sounds

A Mantra is a sound, syllable, word, or words that have the power to transform energy.

Clearing out emotions from the Sacral Center is easily accomplished with sound therapy because it helps you to recognize what you feel. As you allow yourself to feel repressed emotions, you can release them in the most positive way possible. The following sounds are like audial medicine for your Sacral Chakra.

In India's ancient Sanskrit language, the sound of each character corresponds to one or more of the energy centers found in the human body. Most Sanskrit Mantras include a foundational *bija* sound, and the Sanskrit bija healing sound for the Sacral Chakra is *vam*, pronounced as "vum." Practice chanting this sound to yourself in a quiet place and let it become part of your breath. Inhale normally and exhale by chanting this sound, with the emphasis on holding the sound of the last letter of this word.

Another simple sound you can practice saying on each exhalation is *oo*, pronounced the same way you would speak the short vowel sound in the word "move." This syllable has a very soothing effect on the mind and emotions.

You can also repeat the phrase "*I Feel*," which is the statement that embodies the Sacral Chakra. (Remember that this chakra is associated with our birthright to feel and want.)

Did you know that the notes of the C major scale have a therapeutic correspondence to each one of your chakras? The first note, low C, has a healing effect on your Root Chakra, and the second note, D, helps to realign the Sacral Chakra.

Music has a powerful effect on our energy, and every song we hear centers itself around the intricate harmonies of one foundational note that determines the song's key. If you love listening to music, try selecting cheerful classical pieces written in the key of D major, because this key has the most uplifting effect on the spirit of your emotional energy center. Songs in this key include Mozart's Flute Concerto No. 2 in D major, Mozart's Violin Concerto No. 4 in D major, and Johann Pachelbel's Canon in D major.

Since the Sacral Chakra is linked to water, for the best possible use of sound therapy in meditation, meditate beside the ocean. The soothing sound of the ocean waves as they caress the shoreline will have a beneficial effect on your practice. If you life far away from the ocean, download some meditation-friendly ocean sounds, don a pair of headphones, and you'll soon feel as if the ocean were in your bedroom.

For a deeper meditation, match the rhythm of your breathing with that of the ocean. Inhale as the waves recede and exhale slowly when they crash to shore. By altering your breath in this way, you develop a steady rhythm that calms your soul and releases tension from your sacral center.

Foods that Help Activate Your Sacral Chakra

The optimum diet for your sacral center is made up of deeply nourishing foods. The sacral center is the home of the water element inside your body, meaning that making sure that you're drinking enough water each day is critical to keeping it healthy. Most people spend the majority of their lives dehydrated, without ever realizing how much trouble it causes them, and studies estimate that more than half of all headaches in America are due to chronic dehydration.

Try to drink eight standard-size glasses of water daily as part of your routine to stay hydrated and help flush any toxins that accumulate in your system.

The sacral center requires a good supply of healthy oils, which are readily available from most nuts and seeds. Some of the healthiest oil-rich foods include sesame seeds, pumpkin seeds, walnuts, almonds, and hemp seeds. Fish are another good source of healthy oils, and both salmon and trout contain high levels of essential fatty acids that help balance hormones. Coconut oil is one of the healthiest oils you can use; adding coconut oil to some of your favorite recipes is a tasty way to add some extra nutrition to your meals.

Raw, unprocessed honey, nurtures all seven tissues of the body and helps revitalize reproductive organs. Add it to your tea, along with cinnamon and vanilla, for added benefits.

The color orange is also well-known for stimulating the healing of the Sacral Chakra. Nutrient-rich, orange-colored foods include passion fruit, mangoes, yams, sweet potatoes, carrots, pumpkins, papayas, apricots, and oranges. Try snacking on orange-colored fruits as much as possible and avoid highly processed foods that are high in sugar, since they can slow down your body's absorption of precious vitamins and minerals.

These are general food and drink suggestions, please take care to respect your existing food allergies and doctor recommendations.

More Simple Methods to Balance Your Sacral Chakra

Open yourself to pleasure and learn to go with the flow.

You can also encourage positive energy to enter your sacral center in a variety of other ways; the most important thing to remember is to maintain a receptive attitude in your daily life. Attempting to accept things for what they are will allow you to make better life choices. There are so many ways in which we can receive pleasure from our daily life - so long as you remain open to these opportunities and allow yourself to move in the direction of life's natural flow instead of constantly going against it.

Make sure you have a creative outlet.

Everyone needs a creative outlet to express their feelings fully; your outlet could be art, music, dance, writing, or some expressive sport. Try new things and you might be surprised by how much you enjoy your new creative self.

Enjoy the water and moonlight.

Bring new life into your emotional center by spending time in the moonlight. Your sensual pleasure will be greatest on a full-moon night - the Moon's energy is palpable and energizing when you're outside. This is the perfect time to have a romantic dinner outdoors, sit outside by a lake or pond, or swim in an outdoor pool. The ocean waves are generally higher during a full moon, which makes for extra fun if you like to surf or swim at night.

Other activities and environments to stimulate your five senses, especially *touch*, include:

- Steam baths, saunas, and soaking in a Jacuzzi
- Wine-tasting events and classes
- Chocolate-tasting events and classes
- Cooking classes
- Spa sessions - including massage, and beauty treatments like exfoliation
- Painting *mandalas*
- Creative and artistic endeavors, such as writing or singing
- Cultivating or being enclosed in a beautiful environment

- Shaking things up and doing something different, even if it's just a new hairstyle.

Let your intuition guide you as you try out some of these practices to balance your Second Chakra. Remember that change is always possible once you open yourself up to new experiences, and, with the strengthening of your sacral center, you'll gain a new optimism about life.

Specialized Techniques to Clear and Balance Your Sacral Chakra

Passion, intimacy, creativity, and emotional expression are all managed by the wondrous Sacral Chakra! When it is out of balance, you may have difficulty with self-esteem, relationships, and a general feeling of unhappiness.

Luckily, clearing and balancing this important Chakra is possible through many wonderful options and techniques. Many of these advanced techniques can be performed alone with a few simple instructions and materials, but if you feel unsure, you can always reach out to a local, experienced healer for guidance.

What follows are a few more methods for opening and clearing your Sacral Chakra.

Gemstone Therapy

The use of therapeutic crystals and gemstones goes as far back as the ancient cultures and practices of ayurveda, Native American shamanism, and Chinese medicine. It has long been known that crystals and gemstones are healing tools that work through what science calls the piezoelectric effect. These powerful stones respond to the electricity that courses through our body. The vibrations of the stones help to harmonize, balance, and stimulate sluggish or blocked energy channels. Alternative healers all over the world use gemstones today.

When using gemstones, it's recommended that you work slowly and keep a written record of each treatment session. Journaling will help solidify your emotional and spiritual healing. It'll also provide helpful insight as to which stones are suited for your personal purposes.

Preparation:

In order to work with gemstones, you must prepare your mind and surroundings. Begin with a simple meditation, with the intent of clearing your mind of any preconceived notions or doubts. Before you begin your healing ritual, create a sacred space. Keep in mind that you're creating this special moment and place just for you. The more sacred and special the ritual is, the more powerful the effects.

Selecting the Stones:

Below is a helpful list of stones typically used to balance the Sacral Chakra. Before you begin, take each stone individually and hold it in the palm of your hand. Allow yourself to get to know each of the stones. Every one has a separate frequency and offers its own healing vibration.

If you aren't sure which stone you need, simply holding one will present a feeling, letting you know whether it's right for your purposes. If you're working with a healing practitioner, she may have you lie down so she can place gemstones around your body. You can also do this yourself, focusing on the Second Chakra, below the navel.

Sacral Chakra Gemstones:

You'll use gemstones often, especially those that are the same color as the Chakra you wish to balance. The Second Chakra is orange, so in order to balance it, you'll want to choose your stones accordingly.

- *Orange Carnelian* - This is an excellent stone for healing, balance, precision, perception, and eliminating negativity. It's also good for cleansing and activating energy.

- *Fire Opal* – Often known as the "stone of optimism", the fire opal can stimulate enthusiasm and act as a magnet for money or abundance. It also enhances personal power, inner fire, and awakening.

- *Orange Jasper* – Jasper is considered the nurturing stone. It promotes relaxation, comfort, and gentleness. It's a wonderful stone to help you through an emotional trauma and can bring deep emotional healing.

- *Orange Tourmaline* – Tourmaline is widely used in Chakra-balancing. Orange tourmaline enhances creativity and assists with clearing and sexuality.

- *Moonstone* – Moonstone is a powerful stone that stimulates all aspects of femininity. It assists with the menstrual cycle, digestion, cleansing, and reproductive organs. The moonstone can soothe stress and anxiety and connect the Second and Sixth Chakras to create emotional balance and gracefulness.

- *Amber* – Amber is a powerful protector and cleanser. It helps align the mental and emotional bodies and promotes positive mental health. Amber is wonderful for absorbing any negative energies we tend to collect, especially in the Sacral Chakra region.

- *Orange Calcite* – This stone acts as an amplifier and healer, which makes it great for clearing chakras. It is uplifting and encourages joy, happiness, and humor.

Aromatherapy

Aromatherapy, also known as essential oil therapy, is a medium that uses plant extracts and aromas to balance and harmonize the body, mind, and spirit. Have you ever noticed that certain scents awaken particular feelings? You may walk into a room that smells of lavender and immediately feel a sense of relaxation, comfort, or the awakening of a past memory.

Aromatherapy has an effect on the brain's limbic system, which controls emotions and memory function. Basically, when these fragrant oils are inhaled, their scents stimulate the brain to trigger a reaction. Such stimulation causes chemical reactions that can impose a variety of bodily sensations and moods – including relaxation, calm, or excitement.

Using aromatherapy can help stimulate the chakras and bring them back into balance. Essential oils are often used during massage and baths, as a topical application, or for simple inhalation. Many people use a diffuser while relaxing, meditating, or practicing yoga to receive these benefits. When balancing or cleansing the Sacral Chakra, you can use any of the following oils:

- *Citrus Oils* – The smell of citrus sparks memories of the warm, sunny days of summer. Citrus oils can include the essential oils such as neroli, orange and Melissa. Citrus oils invoke an immediate energizing aroma that lifts your spirits. Some of these oils offer complex undertones of sweetness and florals. They are not recommended for topical application but they make wonderful positive mood stimulators when diffused. These oils are calming, soothing, sensual, uplifting, and cheery.

- *Rose* – Rose is one of the most recognizable and oldest essential oils. The scent of roses creates feelings of love and warmth. This oil stimulates romance; it's comforting and gently uplifting.

- *Jasmine* – Jasmine is used again and again in many fragrances and perfumes. It has a full, rich, honey-like sweetness and is a valuable essential oil. Jasmine flowers must be handpicked before dawn, when the flowers' essence is at its peak. Large quantities of flowers are required to produce a small amount of oil. This knowledge can help you use jasmine in an even more sacred manner. Jasmine stimulates feelings of calm, romance, relaxation, and sensuality.

- *Hibiscus* – This oil offers a pleasing aroma that is often used in potpourri or air fresheners. As a healing agent, this plant promotes the opening of pathways through the energetic body. Hibiscus stimulates calm, relaxation, and the movement of energy.

- *Indian Paintbrush* – This lively and dynamic aroma helps stimulate creative energy and passion, opening channels to facilitate artistic flow. It also grounds and energizes the body. Indian paintbrush is also useful in igniting the forces of physical vitality for higher creative work. This essential oil optimizes energy, passion, and creativity.

- *Lady's Slipper* – This delicate orchid is sometimes called the moccasin flower because of its small, moccasin-like shape. Its essential oil is used to correct menopausal imbalances that affect emotions. Lady's slipper relieves anxiety and depression and stimulates reproductive balance.

- *Vanilla* – Long-used and much-loved, vanilla arouses feelings of calm and comfort. Vanilla essential oil offers nurture, balance, and comfort.

- *Sandalwood* – Sandalwood blends nicely with many other essential oils and provides aromatherapy benefits that help center the body, mind, and spirit. It stimulates relaxation, sensuality, and focus.

Yoga Poses

Practicing yoga is another powerful method used to connect our mind and spirit to our body. When our chakras are out of balance, we not only experience deep emotional trauma but also physical pain. Often, holding onto negative energies or not healing these blocks within our spiritual and emotional selves can cause a great deal of physical repercussions. Tension, chronic pain, and illness can all occur when we don't release these past or present blocks.

The Sacral Chakra Asanas (an Asana is the general term for a yoga position) often focus on the movement of the hips and lower abdomen. Some of these poses help with opening this chakra, while others promote the movement of energy to the area. Since the Sacral Chakra is associated with the element of water, and water is the ultimate source of abundance, creative energy, and vitality, the Asanas below are all fluid. When we unlock this Chakra though our physical connection, we will release our most potent creative powers, dreams, and fantasies.

Happy Baby - Ananda Balasana

The Happy Baby pose brings a greater awareness to the hip joints. It's also a great release for the lower back, which is where we tend to lock many emotions and much tension (and don't you just love the name?).

1. Arrange a yoga mat or folded blanket on the floor. Lie down on you back and, while you exhale, bring your needs towards your chest.

2. While you inhale, grab the outsides of your feet or hold onto a belt looped over your feet (you can also hold onto your ankles if gripping your feet is too difficult and you don't have a belt handy). Place each of your ankles over the knee of the same side, making

sure your shins are at a 90-degree angle to each thigh. Exhale and gentle push your feet against your hand (or belts).

3. Press your tailbone toward the floor and lengthen your spine (including your neck).

4. While exhaling, open your knees a bit wider than your torso and move them up in the direction of your armpits, trying to keep your ankles above your knees.

5. Hold for one minute and then release the pose, bringing your knees to your chest, then exhaling and bringing your feet back to the floor.

Lizard Pose – Utthan Pristhasana

The Lizard pose is another hip-opening Asana that can help release negative emotions, such as guilt, fear, and sadness. It's also great for stretching the thighs and hamstrings.

1. From Downward Facing Dog, step the right foot outside of the right hand.

2. Bring both forearms to the floor in front of you, inside the right leg.

3. Keep your inner left thigh lifted.

4. Press the heel away, focusing on the spine's natural extension.

Keep the hips square.

5. Hold for five breaths and repeat on the other side.

Revolved Abdomen Pose – Jathara Parivartanasana

The Revolved Abdomen pose is wonderful for releasing toxins and emotional fatigue. It also decompresses the spine, where we have a habit of storing a lot of emotional baggage. This pose is an effective way to stretch the hips and promote energy movement to the Sacral Chakra.

1. Begin by lying on your back with your knees bent and your feet flat on the floor. You may wish to keep your head on a pillow to support your neck.

2. Slowly bring your knees to your chest and wrap your hands around them, breathing with intention and awareness.

3. Allow your arms to rest, palms down, at your side.

4. As you exhale, lower your legs to the left (keeping your knees), twisting the spine and allowing your right hip to lift off the floor. Allow the left foot to rest on the ground.

5. If possible, bring your torso and legs into a 90-degree angle.

6. Turn your head right while keeping the shoulder blades pressed down toward the floor and away from your ears.

7. Hold for several breaths, then release slowly by centering your feet and raising them toward the ceiling. Bend your knees toward your chest.

8. Repeat the steps on the other side.

Goddess Squat – Kaliasana

Also known as the Victory Squat, this pose opens the hips and chest, providing warm, energetic movement between chakras. It is also very beneficial for women who are pregnant and preparing for childbirth.

1. Begin by standing with your feet about 3 feet apart (or a little less).

2. Bend your elbows and bring your palms facing one other and meeting in the center of your chest.

3. Rotate your feet out 15-30 degrees and bend your knees, squatting down and exhaling over the toes. Try to keep your knees over your ankles.

4. Let your pelvic floor drop while releasing tension in that area. Keep you spine straight and long.

5. Breathe and continue holding for five breaths.

6. Inhale and straighten your legs, reaching your fingertips toward

the ceiling. Exhale and bring your arms to your sides.

Cobra Pose – Bhujangasana

The Cobra pose is a very powerful Asana. It can help relieve depression, anxiety, and stress, as well as any discomfort in the muscles of the back, abdomen, and neck.

1. Lie on your stomach, placing your toes flat on the floor. Rest your forehead on the floor.

2. With your palms down, place your hands under your shoulders, keeping your elbows parallel and close to your torso.

3. Inhale and slowly lift your head, chest, and abdomen while keeping your navel pressed to the floor.

4. If possible, straighten your arms and arch your back. Tilt your head back and look upward.

5. Exhale and gently lower your torso back to the floor.

MORE ADVANCED POSITIONS FOR BALANCING THE SACRAL CHAKRA

If you are an advanced student of yoga, you may also want to try a few additional Asanas that are more challenging.

Eagle Pose – Garudasana

This challenging pose allows your body to stretch in many directions and provides excellent release in the groin and sacrum, where many people hold tension. It also allows a free flow of energy into the lower body. However, you should not practice this pose if you have had a recent knee injury or suffer from balance problems. Practice this pose against a wall for additional safety.

Cow Face Pose – Gomukhasana

The Cow Face creates a wonderful balance between the body's left and right side. It stretches almost every part of the body and helps increase blood and energy flow through the body, relieving fatigue, stress, and anxiety.

Pigeon Pose – Eka Pada Rajakapotasana

Otherwise knows as the One-Legged King Pigeon pose, this Asana is a wonderful Sacral Chakra-opener. It focuses on widening and opening the hips, shoulders, and spine.

It is important to always consult with your doctor before attempting yoga positions.

Through these advanced healing techniques, you will bring about a transformation that will depend on how you relate to your energy systems. These methods will bring greater awareness and intuition in terms of your emotional tendencies and blockages. Soon, you'll be able to fine-tune the practices that work best for your body and find your Sacral Chakra opening to receive this wonderful healing energy.

Common Questions about Chakra-Balancing Techniques

Chakra-balancing is the surest and safest way to physical, emotional, and spiritual well-being. Balanced chakras place you at the center of the energetic exchange, both within and without. These techniques require little more than positive intention and focused breathing; no drugs, stethoscopes, or X-rays are required to access the limitless bounty of chakra balance! In fact, techniques to align your chakras - and keep them aligned - are so applicable and practical that anyone can do them.

However, many people have questions regarding the effectiveness and safety of these techniques. Here are some questions commonly asked by those who are new to chakra-healing techniques.

How long and how often should I practice these balancing techniques?

Practice them every day for ten to thirty minutes, or up to an hour. Daily practice keeps the energy circulating smoothly, without blockages, and will keep a person fit, healthy, and happy, stimulating overall longevity and vitality. Beginners can start with ten minutes and work their way up to thirty. Ideally, you shouldn't practice these techniques for more than an hour. More than that is probably unnecessary, unless your intuition or health condition suggests otherwise. Performing these exercises once a day will prevent sickness, enhance energy reserves, and promote mental clarity and emotional stability.

Whether or not you should exercise these techniques more than once a day depends on whether you suffer from a sever illness or imbalance. Practicing two or three times a day is usually recommended for those who are trying to heal a serious imbalance. Those who suffer from chronic illnesses or degenerative diseases usually fall into this category.

It's important to understand that chakras can't be in perfect alignment all of the time. This is an evolutionary process. It's more of a spiritual unfolding than a state of perfect health. Nonetheless, we should strive for alignment because it is through the balance of our chakras that we reach spiritual clarity, which, in turn, gives us optimal physical and emotional health.

What happens if I do the techniques incorrectly?

It's practically impossible to perform these techniques incorrectly. You can only expect positive side effects from practicing meditations and visualizations. So long as you focus on the affirmations of love, joy, healing, and abundance - and not their absence - there won't be any negative side effects. Mediation and visualization are soft tools with a big impact, and their consistent use will only benefit you in limitless ways.

Now, if you are doing the more physical exercises, such as yoga for chakra-balancing, practice some care and common sense. Never try to force yourself. The results could, in fact, turn out to be negative, painful and you could end up really hurting yourself!

In addition, striving to unlock the Kundalini energy, for anyone experienced in these techniques, is typically not a dangerous goal to pursue, but, because the surge of energy that comes forth can be overwhelming, caution is always advised.

Chakra-balancing is a personal healing art that requires consistency. There's no need to perform these practices excessively; healing is a gradual process. Chakra balance must be constantly realized, and you'll become more in-tune with these techniques as you practice. You'll eventually begin to intuit what works for you and what doesn't, and you can work with your intuition accordingly.

APPENDIX - A Brief Explanation of the Seven Chakras

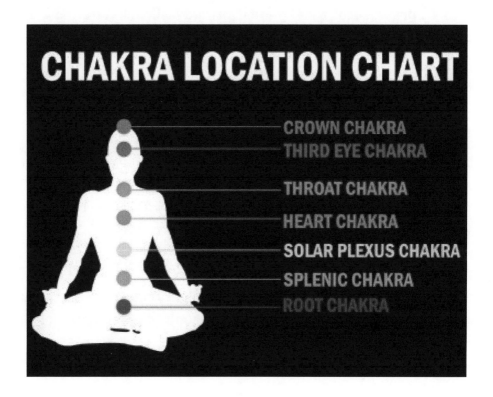

To view this chart in full color, please visit:

http://openyourchakras.com/chakralocationchart/

The First Chakra, the Root or Base Chakra, is a deep, rich red. It is literally located at the base of the spine. The Universal Life Force energy or chi enters the body here, through the Root Chakra, and moves upward until it reaches the Crown Chakra at the top of the head.

The First Chakra roots us to the Earth to support our survival and provide grounding. When the First Chakra is in balance, we feel secure and aware at the most basic level. We can give and receive love and provide for all our body's physical needs - food, shelter, clothing, and survival.

Out of balance, this chakra could express its condition with issues such as being ungrounded, fear of moving forward in life, general anxiety, and addiction. Physically, the body might respond with pain, brain fog, colitis, diarrhea, or menopausal symptoms.

The Second Chakra is called the Sacral; it connects to the sacrum, located just below the navel, behind the genitals. Its color is orange-red. It is the lower emotional aspect addressing earthly and bodily emotions.

From here, the Sacral Chakra drives creativity, joy, sensual urges, and sexuality. Promiscuity and lack of sex drive are both imbalances of the Second Chakra. This is also the home of the "gut feeling," where we admit we know things but have no reason for our certainty. That feeling is the result of the dual aspect of spiritual energies coming from the Crown Chakra and interacting with the base energies of our grounding with Earth in the Root Chakra. We are naturally balanced here, expanding recognition and acceptance of our dual nature, allowing us to enjoy a strong spiritual and physical mindset.

This is also the spiritual home of all impressions and feelings. When people can't deal with feelings of guilt and humiliation, they often store those negative feelings here. Holding all of that negative emotion here is damaging, impairing the healthy flow of energy to the next chakra and, worse, creating fear of and disgust with ourselves.

The Third Chakra, following the progression of the prism or rainbow, shines a clear yellow or the yellow-green purity of newly sprouted plant shoots. It is found at the solar plexus, just above the naval. Universal Life Energy flows strongest into this chakra, affecting our feelings about everything. Health and happiness are the rewards of balancing this chakra.

The Third Chakra affects two divergent aspects of the mind: depending upon the state of the Third Chakra, the mind can be focused on maintaining willpower or it can be lost to apathy. Since ideas and assimilation are controlled here, it is a manifest power center – or not – depending on your choices and actions.

An imbalance will result in fear and anger in your pursuits, but, when in balance, your confidence and purpose will shine the pure golden yellow of the Sun on your dreams and point to the road for success.

The Fourth Chakra is a fresh, bright green or sometimes a rose red. It is found at the physical heart and its balance is essential for healing. It is the seat of love, respect, compassion, happiness, self-esteem, and surrender.

As the Center of all Chakras, it is also the connection through which all energy flows in either direction. Here earthly energies are converting both to and from the spiritual energies. Unconditional love and the desire to care for ourselves and others flow out from here. It is the seat of our empathetic nature and sympathy.

The Fifth Chakra, found at the throat, is the first of our energy spiritual centers, and it has no connection to our earthly plane. Resonating as the pure blue of lapis, it is our gateway to self-expression, honesty and decision-making. Professional capability or an excess of pride and blaming others are among the consequences of the Fifth Chakra's balance or imbalance.

The Sixth Chakra is well known as the Third Eye. Its color is the deep blue of indigo. Located in the center of our forehead, it is the place where we find our intuition, insight and understanding. Psychic ability flows from here. The all-important mind-body connection can be accessed and strengthened here. Clairvoyance, as well as our understanding of things, depends on the balance of this chakra.

The Seventh Chakra sits as the top of our heads. It is also the area enclosed by a sovereign crown, which is why it became known as the

Crown Chakra. Our ultimate spiritual connection and the integration of our physical, mental, emotional, and spiritual wholeness lie here in this center.

About The Author

Mirtha Contreras was attracted to everything related to personal growth and spirituality for as long as she can remember. She began her professional training as a rebirther nearly twenty years ago before she went on to create her own rebirthing school, where both her career and personal growth studies began to flourish. Mirtha's interest in how the emotional intertwines with the energetic grew over the years, and she went on to be trained as a teacher in Spiritual Response Therapy.

Over the years, Mirtha has helped hundreds of clients and students, using her skills as a Reiki Master, facilitator of the EMF Balancing Technique®, Systemic Family Therapist (Family Constellations), trained practitioner of The Reconnection and Reconnective Healing, and as facilitator of the Mindful Self-Awareness technique. She has also appeared as an expert guest on numerous television and radio shows.

Every step she has taken on her career path is driven by her enthusiasm to serve those who wish to learn more about managing their emotional state and the energetic power needed to shift consciousness and harness personal strength.

Mirtha strives to help people become aware of their own inner power in order to increase their confidence as they recognize that we are all able to overcome any obstacle and achieve our goals - and she aims to do so with the best attitude and disposition. For Mirtha, witnessing these changes is the most fulfilling aspect of her work.

Thank You!

Thank you so much for purchasing this book!

I really hope you enjoyed it as much as I enjoyed writing it. I am dedicated to making sure I produce something valuable to my readers.

If you feel I've succeeded, would you please be so kind as to leave a review on Amazon, on the product page where you purchased this book?

By doing so, you can help me reach more people!

I wish you peace, love, and many blessings.

-Mirtha

www.OpenYourChakras.com

7962684R00056

Printed in Germany
by Amazon Distribution
GmbH, Leipzig